D1137276

Sugar Inspirations

Sugar Quilting

NADENE HURST

MEREHURST

Dedication

To my granddaughter, Julia

First published 1997 by Merehurst Limited
Ferry House, 51–57 Lacy Road, Putney,
London SW15 1PR

Copyright © Merehurst Limited 1997
ISBN 1-85391-660-9

A catalogue record for this book is available from the
British Library.

Editor: Helen Southall
Design: Anita Ruddell
Photography by Sue Atkinson

Colour separation by Bright Arts, Hong Kong
Printed in Hong Kong by Wing King Tong

Contents

Introduction

Based on needlecraft techniques, sugar quilting is a new and very effective method of cake decorating.

The idea for the techniques used to decorate the cakes in this book came to me several years ago when I viewed an exhibition on the art of needlework quilting. Translating this into sugar produced the effects you see. The beauty of sugar quilting lies in its simplicity: here is something new for the experienced cake decorator, but it is also something that the beginner can attempt without too much difficulty.

Because of the adaptability of this method of decoration, the designs are easily accommodated on cakes of various sizes and shapes, although this might result in some alteration to the side pattern.

Equipment and Materials

The following are used throughout this book. Special items required for specific tasks are detailed where relevant.

Stitch wheels

Two sizes of stitch wheel are required: the small one is incorporated in the quilting tool, and the larger one is included in the designer wheel set. In the instructions for the designs in this book, these will often be referred to simply as 'large stitch' and 'small stitch'.

Perspex sheets

For most of the designs in this book, the basic pattern is impressed into the sugarpaste using a sheet of perspex on to which the pattern has been piped in royal icing. Sheets of perspex can be bought from sign-makers and DIY shops. It needs to be fairly thin (about 2.5mm/⅛ inch thick), but not flexible. If the perspex is too thick, the pattern becomes distorted through it and is difficult to pipe. If it is flexible, the pip-

ing can break away when the perspex is bent. Small sheets of glass can be used as an alternative.

Whenever possible, use a piece of perspex slightly larger than the size of the cake; this avoids making marks in the paste around the edges. With practice and care, smaller pieces can be used for separate lettering, if required.

Most side designs should be piped at the bottom edge of the perspex so that you can use them at any level, or they can be piped at a set distance from the base of the cake. They require a piece of perspex that is longer than the pattern to enable you to hold the perspex against the side of the cake whilst impressing.

Basic equipment

You will also need: large and small non-stick rolling pins, non-stick board, turntable, sugar dredger, scalpel, small sharp knife, rulers of various widths and lengths, pencil, tracing paper, piping tubes (tips), piping bags, scissors, palette knife with 10cm (4 inch) blade, plastic side scraper, masking tape, desk lamp, confectioners' varnish and food colouring.

Paste

All the sugarpaste (rolled fondant) used in this book is commercially produced, and is obtainable from specialist cake decoration shops and supermarkets. Flower paste is also used, and can be bought ready-made. Alternatively, you can use the recipe given on page 6.

Varnish

Confectioners' varnish has been used in small amounts on some of the cakes. This is an edible product available from sugarcraft shops, and although it has a very strong smell when wet, it is tasteless when dry. If you wish to keep a design piped on perspex for continuous use, brush over the dry royal icing with confectioners' varnish.

Techniques

The basic techniques of sugar quilting are incorporated in the instructions for the Blossom Cake on pages 7–11.

Colouring

Some sugarpaste is available ready-coloured; it can be used alone or mixed with white to make other tints. This is particularly useful for the base covering on a cake, saving the time and effort needed to colour large amounts of paste. Other colours can be achieved by mixing in paste or liquid food colours.

Where a large amount of paste has to be coloured, first mix the colouring thoroughly into a small lump of paste, then add this to the remainder. This helps to avoid thin streaks of colour appearing, which are difficult to disperse. Remember that colours fade rapidly in daylight; always keep coloured cakes in a dark cupboard or a lidded box when you are not working on them.

Basic Recipes

Flower Paste

Once made, store this paste carefully in a polythene bag in an airtight container in the fridge. Alternatively, it can be frozen.

500g (1lb/3cups) icing (confectioners') sugar, sifted
3 teaspoons gum tragacanth
2 teaspoons powdered gelatine
5 teaspoons hot water
2 teaspoons liquid glucose
2 teaspoons white vegetable fat (shortening)
1 egg white, lightly beaten

1 Sift the icing sugar and gum tragacanth together into the bowl of an electric food mixer, and warm.

2 Sprinkle the gelatine on to the water in a heatproof bowl, and leave for 5-10 minutes to 'sponge'. Place over a pan of hot water to dissolve.

3 Add the liquid glucose and fat to the gelatine and stir until dissolved. Add this mixture and the lightly beaten egg white to the icing sugar. Blend together, then beat with the mixer for about 5 minutes until white and stringy. Gather together and place in a polythene bag.

Royal Icing

This is required for piping patterns on to perspex, and for making padding using a thick runny sugar consistency, piped directly on to the sugarpaste.

2 tablespoons dried egg white or substitute
4 tablespoons water
500g (1lb/3 cups) icing (confectioners') sugar

1 Dissolve the egg white powder in the water. Strain into the bowl of an electric mixer and add the icing sugar.

2 Combine the ingredients and beat on the slowest speed until the icing stands up in peaks.

3 Alternatively, if making by hand, dissolve the egg white powder in the water and strain into a bowl, then add the icing sugar in spoonfuls, beating between each one, until the correct consistency is reached.

Blossom Cake

This cake uses the basic techniques of sugar quilting, those that follow incorporate variations and additional ideas. The design is suitable for an 18–23cm (7–9 inch) cake and is easily adapted for many occasions by adding lettering.

Materials

Royal icing
18cm (7 inch) round cake
25cm (10 inch) round cake board
750g (1½ lb) marzipan (almond paste)
750g (1½ lb) sugarpaste (rolled fondant)
Pink, purple, green, brown and yellow food colourings
Ribbon to trim board

Equipment

Piping bags
Nos. 1.5 and 2 piping tubes (tips)
Serrated open-scallop crimper

Piping the design

1 Trace the pattern (page 41) on to a piece of paper the same size and shape as the top of the cake. Place the tracing face up on top of a piece of perspex, and secure with masking tape.

2 Turn the perspex over and pipe the design in white royal icing directly on to the perspex using a no. 1.5 tube for the flower, buds and leaves, and a no. 2 tube for the stems. (Always use a tube that is one size larger when you wish to pipe into the impressed groove, e.g. for lettering, lines and stems.) As you pipe, try to keep the joins neat as untidy joins will result in holes showing on the sugarpaste. If you find it difficult to create good joins, leave a gap instead, and complete the groove on the cake using the veining end of the quilting tool.

3 Leave the icing to dry, then remove the paper pattern from the perspex.

Covering the cake

4 Before covering the cake, make sure you have all the necessary equipment ready; the impressions need to be made as soon as the cake is covered, while the sugarpaste is still soft. Place the cake on the board and

cover with marzipan, and then with pale pink sugarpaste.

Quilting lines

5 Impress a line across the centre of the cake using the edge of a ruler. To find the centre line, cut out a piece of paper the same size as the cake top, fold it in half, making a crease across the centre, open it out and place it on top of the cake. Use this as a guide when marking your first line.

6 Continue marking lines, the ruler's width apart, until you have covered the top of the cake. Impress a second set of lines at 90° to the first. (Never make a line on the very edge of the cake, as this will be difficult to extend down the sides.)

7 Using a shorter ruler, extend each line over the rounded edge of the cake, down the side to the base. This is easier performed in two operations,

ensuring that the side lines are straight.

8 Place the perspex pattern, piped side down, on top of the cake. Make sure the design is correctly positioned and that none of the piped lines lie along a quilting line. Press firmly on the perspex, directly over the piping. Do not try to impress by pushing on the edges of the perspex as this may result in the outline of the perspex showing on the sugarpaste, and the

centre of the design not being impressed firmly enough.

> **9** Using the large stitch wheel, impress along the parallel lines marked on the cake in steps 5–7, carefully avoiding the areas which will be covered by the pattern.

> **10** Crimp around the base of the cake, resting the rubber band of the crimper on the board as you proceed. This keeps the crimping just above the edge, and allows for the covering of the board.

Covering the board

> **11** Brush the board with water and cut a strip of pink sugarpaste to fit. Lay this around the cake, pushing it into the base for a neat finish. (On a larger cake you may need to use several shorter strips, then pinch the joins together and smooth the paste.) Trim to the edge of the board and crimp to match the base of the cake.

Padding

> **12** For the padding, place a small amount of royal icing on a plastic side scraper and add a little water until it reaches a thick run-sugar consistency. Place this in a piping bag without a tube and cut off the end to make a small hole.

> **13** Pipe the pads on the design, covering the areas within the broken lines shown on the pattern (page 41). A margin is left around the edge of each padded area to allow room for the covering. (Not all parts of a design need to be padded; leaving some of the background sections unpadded adds depth to the overall effect. Side motifs are also left unpadded.)

> **14** Dry the run-sugar under direct heat, such as a desk lamp, for about 1 hour. This quick drying will prevent the sugar sinking.

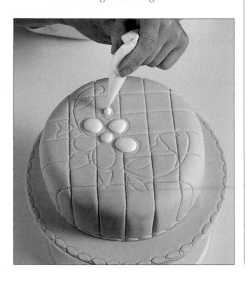

15 Leave the cake to dry naturally for 24 hours until the sugarpaste has hardened.

Quilting

16 Colour some small amounts of paste green, yellow and two shades of purple. Each part of the design is cut out and worked separately, except where two small areas of the same colour are adjacent, when it may be possible to cut them out together, but it becomes more difficult to stretch the covering over the padding in all directions.

17 Roll out the paste to about 2.5mm (⅛ inch) thick. Use the original piped design on the perspex to impress the outline of the part needed in the sugarpaste. Cut out using a scalpel. Place the cut piece flat on the work surface and smooth down the edges all around so that they are flat to the surface.

18 With water, dampen around the edges on the back and place the piece on the relevant section of the design on the cake, smoothing the paste down into the surrounding groove. If there is padding underneath, press lightly in the centre to squeeze the paste outwards and stretch it over the pad. (If you press the paste out at the edges to meet the groove, instead of pressing from the centre, you will probably be able to see the outline of the run-sugar underneath.)

19 Using the small wheel on the quilting tool, apply stitching all around, as close to the edge as possible, on each piece as you complete it. (If you leave it until you have done several you might find that the paste has dried and the stitching will be difficult.)

20 For the flower, start with the centre and complete the stitches around this, even though you will be adding petals all around. When stitching around the petals, the wheel will fit into the holes already made around the flower centres.

21 Extra stitch lines can be added for greater effect, across and radiating from the centre of the flower, and as veining on the leaves.

To complete

22 With a no. 1.5 tube, pipe a line of brown royal icing into the grooves of the stems. Trim the board with ribbon.

Orchid Cake

This is a useful design, suitable for many occasions. It incorporates single diagonal quilting and strip crimping around the board.

Materials

Royal icing
18cm (7 inch) round cake
25cm (10 inch) round cake board
750g (1½ lb) marzipan (almond paste)
750g (1½ lb) sugarpaste (rolled fondant)
Green, pink, mauve, brown and yellow food colourings
Ribbon to trim board

Equipment

Piping bags
Nos. 1.5 and 2 piping tubes (tips)
7mm (⅓ inch) strip cutter
Serrated closed-curve crimper

Piping the design

1 Trace the design (page 46), and pipe on to perspex using white royal icing and a no. 1.5 tube. Pipe the curved line with a no. 2 tube. Leave to dry.

Quilting lines

2 Place the cake on the board and cover with marzipan and then with pale green sugarpaste. Cut out a 15cm (6 inch) circle of grease-proof paper, fold it in half, creasing it across the centre, open it out and place it on top of the cake. Use this as a guide to indent a line in the sugarpaste across the centre of the cake with the edge of a ruler.

3 Remove the paper and indent two more parallel lines on either side of the centre line, spacing them the ruler's width apart. Using a smaller ruler, extend the lines over the edge and down to the base of the cake.

4 Using the piped pattern on the perspex, indent the design over the lines, making sure that the lines lie in a diagonal slant in relation to the orchid.

5 Impress large stitches along the straight quilting lines, avoiding the areas covered by the orchid design and the curved line.

6 Indent a line around the base of the cake by resting the ruler on the board and pressing the top edge into the cake. Deepen the groove with the veining end of the quilting tool and impress large stitches along the line. Adding this horizontal line will create four squares at the base of the cake on opposite sides.

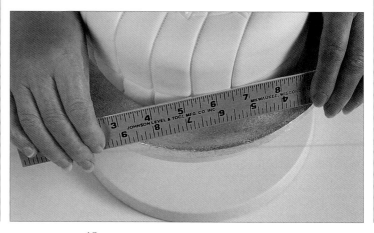

Padding

⬦**7** Using white royal icing of a thick run-sugar consistency, pipe the quilting pads on the sepals and petals of the orchid, keeping the icing within the areas indicated by the dotted lines on the pattern (page 46). On the trumpet of the flower, pipe the pad in a horseshoe shape. Do not pipe the leaves. Place under a desk lamp to dry for 1 hour.

Base of cake

⬦**8** Cut a strip of pink paste, using the ruler as a guide, and cover the longest areas plus

the two centre squares on both sides. Cover the remaining squares with mauve paste. Impress large stitching along the top and down between each section.

⬦**9** Cover the board around the cake with pale green sugarpaste. Cut narrow strips of dark green paste using a strip cutter, and attach around the edge of the board. Crimp.

Quilting

⬦**10** Cover the orchid sepals with pink paste, small stitch around the edges and impress one line down the centre of each. Cover the two petals with mauve, small stitch around the edges and impress two lines down the centre of each. Cover the trumpet, and press into the hollow with your finger to create an indent. Small stitch around

the edge, and impress short stitch lines inwards from the bottom edge to represent the frilling.

⬦**11** Cut out a small oval of thin yellow paste, place on the trumpet and small stitch around. To make the column, roll a small cone of mauve paste, indent the sides at the rounded end with the small stitch wheel, and place on top of the yellow area.

⬦**12** Using green paste, cover the leaves, small stitch around the edges, and mark in veins.

To complete

⬦**13** Using a no. 1.5 tube, pipe a line of brown royal icing into the curved groove on top of the cake. Trim the board with ribbon.

Ribbons and Bows

This pretty cake is easily adapted to any occasion by altering the decoration on the central plaque. The quilted bow design is extended down the side of the cake.

Materials

Flower paste
1kg (2lb) sugarpaste (rolled fondant)
Selection of petal dusts (blossom tints), optional
Royal icing
Pink, mauve, green, yellow and brown food colourings
15x23cm (6x9 inch) oval cake
23x30cm (9x12 inch) oval cake board
1kg (2lb) marzipan (almond paste)
Ribbon to trim board

Equipment

Oval plaque cutter (about 7.5x11.5cm/3x4 inches)
Airbrush, optional
Piping bags
Nos. 0, 1, 1.5, 2, 3 and 50 piping tubes (tips)
Embroidery pins (4cm/1½ inch curve and flower), optional

Plaque

1 Make up some paste using equal amounts of flower paste and sugarpaste (about 30g/1oz of each). Roll out thinly and cut out an oval plaque. Leave to dry.

2 Trace or scribe the flower design (page 42) on to the plaque. Using an airbrush or petal dust mixed with cornflour, colour the surface to match the piping which will lie over the top (mauve behind the lupins, pink behind the other flowers, green for the leaves and brown behind the stems). If using petal dust, fix the colour by placing the plaque upside-down in a metal sieve and passing through a jet of steam.

3 Pipe the design with royal icing in the following sequence. Lupins (no. 0 tube, mauve icing): Commence piping at the top with tiny bulbs, increasing the size towards the base of the stem. Leaves (no. 50 tube, pale green icing): Apply light, even pressure when piping the centre and top leaves. For the bottom leaves, apply extra pressure at the beginning to

make a wider base, then taper off to a fine point. Flowers (no. 2 tube, deep pink icing): Soften the icing slightly to create a smooth bulb. Pipe the petals with bulbs, pulled to a short point towards the centre of the flower. Using a no. 0 tube and yellow icing, pipe tiny bulbs in the centre of each flower. Finally, pipe the stems at the base of the design with a no. 1 tube and brown icing.

Ribbons and bows

4 Trace the ribbon and bows design (page 42), and pipe on to perspex using white royal icing and a no. 1.5 tube. Trace and pipe the side tails on a separate smaller piece of perspex. Leave to dry.

5 Place the cake on the board and cover with marzipan and then with pale pink sugarpaste. Using the plaque cutter, cut through the paste in the centre of the top of the cake and remove the paste. Replace with the decorated plaque and smooth the paste around the edges.

6 Use the piped ribbon and bow template to impress the design around the top of the cake, and extend by placing the tails template under each knot and rocking it over the edge and down the side of the cake.

7 Cover the board around the cake with sugarpaste. Soften down some pink sugarpaste with water to a piping consistency, and pipe a continu-

ous pearl around the base of the cake with a no. 3 tube.

Padding

8 Using white royal icing of a thick run-sugar consistency, pipe the padding on the top of the cake in the areas indicated by the dotted lines on the pattern (page 42). Leave to dry under a desk lamp.

Quilting

9 Cover the ribbons and bows with paste that is a slightly deeper pink than the cake covering. Roll out to 2.5mm (⅛ inch) thick, impress with the perspex pattern and cut out all the sections separately. Work on one piece at a time, keeping the other pieces covered.

10 Smooth down and moisten the edges, and place each

piece over its pad. Press down into place and small stitch around the edges. Work around the top of the cake until completed, using the small stitch wheel to impress lines on the bows to indicate folds as you go along.

11 Cover the tails, this time without padding underneath. Small stitch around the edges and on top to give the impression of folds.

To complete

12 Scribe the embroidery design on the board, below the tails of each bow, or use embroidery pins if you have them, inserting a 4cm (1½ inch) curve below a flower pin. Pipe the design using the same tubes and colours as for the top plaque. Trim the board with pale pink ribbon.

Twin Teddies

For this design, the quilting effect is extended to the board.

Materials

Royal icing
20cm (8 inch) square cake
28cm (11 inch) square cake board
1kg (2lb) marzipan (almond paste)
1kg (2lb) sugarpaste (rolled fondant)
Pink, blue, brown and cream food colourings
Ribbon to trim board

Equipment

Piping bags
No. 1.5 piping tube (tip)
Blossom cutters
Small heart cutter
7mm (⅛ inch) strip cutter
Serrated open-curve crimper

Piping the design

1 Trace the design (page 45), and pipe on to perspex using a no. 1.5 tube and royal icing, extending the lines to the edge of the perspex.

Quilting lines

2 Place the cake on the board and cover with marzipan. Cover the cake and board with white sugarpaste. Impress with the teddy design.

3 Using a ruler, extend the lines from the corners of the square over the edge of the cake, down the sides and across to the edge of the board. Impress extra lines until the cake and board are divided into squares. Large stitch along all these lines.

Padding and quilting

4 Using royal icing of a thick run-sugar consistency, pipe the padding on the teddies as indicated by the dotted lines on the pattern (page 45). Leave to dry under a desk lamp.

5 Roll out some brown and cream paste and mark with the perspex pattern. Cut out each section separately. Smooth down and moisten all the edges, and cover the pads, commencing with the bodies and working outwards. Apply small stitches to each section. Add eyes, noses and bow ties to the teddies.

Patches

6 To create different coloured patches on the quilting, roll out the paste thinly, cut a square patch and wet around the edges on the back. Place the patch over a square of quilting, pressing the edges into the stitch grooves. Re-apply the large stitching around the edges. Apply larger patches to the corners of the board.

7 To insert patterns in some patches, position the patch, then cut out a blossom shape and replace with a blossom in a contrasting colour. Small stitch each blossom into the centre. Decorate other quilting squares with large cut-out hearts or blossoms.

8 Apply narrow strips of blue paste along the edges of the board and crimp. Trim the board with ribbon.

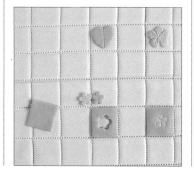

Elephant at Play

This charming cake is suitable for a toddler's birthday.

Materials

Royal icing
25x30cm (10x12 inch) oblong cake
30x36cm (12x14 inch) oblong cake board
1.5kg (3lb) marzipan (almond paste)
1.5kg (3lb) pale lemon sugarpaste (rolled fondant)
Red, blue, mauve, green, yellow, brown and peach food colourings
Confectioners' varnish

Equipment

Piping bags
Nos. 1.5 and 3 piping tubes (tips)
Serrated diamond-shaped crimper

Piping the design

1 Trace the design (page 43), and pipe on to perspex with a no. 1.5 tube and white royal icing.

Quilting lines

2 Place the cake on the cake board and cover with marzipan and pale lemon sugarpaste. For the background quilting lines, start by impressing two diagonal lines, from corner to corner, both ways across the top of the cake.

3 Using these lines as a guide, mark in the rest of the lines parallel to them, spacing them the ruler's width apart. Continue the lines over the edge of the cake just enough to complete each diamond shape, then, from each point, mark down the side of the cake to the base. Mark a line around the base of the cake by resting the ruler on the board and pressing the top edge into the cake.

4 Impress the elephant pattern over the quilting lines on top of the cake. Large stitch along all the quilting lines, avoiding the picture. Cover the board with sugarpaste and crimp.

Padding and quilting

5 Using white royal icing of a thick run-sugar consistency, pipe the padding on the design in the areas indicated by the dotted lines on the pattern (page 43). Dry under a lamp.

6 Roll out some red sugarpaste thinly, and cut strips using the width of the ruler as a guide. Place around the base of the cake, pressing the top edge into the groove already there. Continue the large stitches down the sides over this band and large stitch top and bottom.

7 Cover the elephant in peach sugarpaste, cutting out and working on each section separately. Begin with the ear and the top of the front leg, and work outwards. Add the blue foot pads and a small circle for the eye, and indent with the end of a paintbrush. The saddle is placed over the peach body. Use the small stitch wheel to mark the toes, mouth, eyebrow and ear.

8 Cover the rest of the picture, and use the stitch wheel to add extra pattern to the bricks and doll. Add two brown spots of paste for the eyes and red spots for the cheeks. (These are cut out using a no. 3 tube; to make the cheek circles bigger, press to spread the shape before applying.) Impress buttons down the front of the doll.

To complete

9 Brush the top design with confectioners' varnish, and trim the board with ribbon.

20

Tartan Cake

This colourful design is created using quilted strips without padding underneath.

Materials

1kg (2lb) sugarpaste (rolled fondant)
Egg yellow, green, red, navy and purple food colourings
18cm (7 inch) square cake
25cm (10 inch) square cake board
1kg (2lb) marzipan (almond paste)
Flower paste
Ribbon to trim board

Equipment

4cm (1½ inch) wide ruler
5mm (¼ inch) strip cutter

Preparation

1 Colour 875g (1¾lb) sugarpaste egg yellow, and the remainder purple.

2 Place the cake on the board and cover with marzipan and yellow sugarpaste.

Quilting lines

3 Using the ruler, impress a line 1cm (½ inch) in from each top edge of the cake, then another the ruler's width within and parallel to the first. Continue these lines down the sides.

4 Imprint large stitches along all the quilting lines. Leave to dry.

Tartan pattern

5 Colour half the remaining yellow paste green. Roll this out to 2.5mm (⅛ inch) thick, and cut two strips as wide as the ruler and long enough to go across the cake and down the sides.

6 Smooth down the edges and attach to the cake, using the quilting lines as a guide. Large stitch along all the edges, and across where the strips cross on the corners.

7 Repeat the process with the purple paste, this time making the strips shorter to fit between the green strips and down the sides of the cake. Large stitch the edges.

8 Mix a small amount of equal quantities of sugarpaste and flower paste. Colour some red and some navy. Roll out the navy thinly and cut with a strip cutter. Overlay two strips of navy on each of the green and purple sections, crossing on the corner squares. Leave equal spaces between the lines and on either side. It is necessary to cut a section at a time and join where the large stitching crosses.

9 Roll out and cut red strips, and attach centrally between the navy, again crossing at the corners. Leave to dry.

The board

10 Gather together all the paste that is left, including the yellow, marble it together and roll out. Cut in strips and lay along the board on each side of the cake, overlapping at the corners. Gently push the paste inwards until it fits snugly up to the cake. This overcomes the difficulty of working against different thicknesses of paste where the strips meet the board.

11 Cut through both pieces of overlapped paste on the corners, diagonally from the corner of the cake to the corner of the board. Pinch the paste together and smooth over. Finally, smooth all round the board, taking care not to damage the ends of the strips. Trim the board with ribbon.

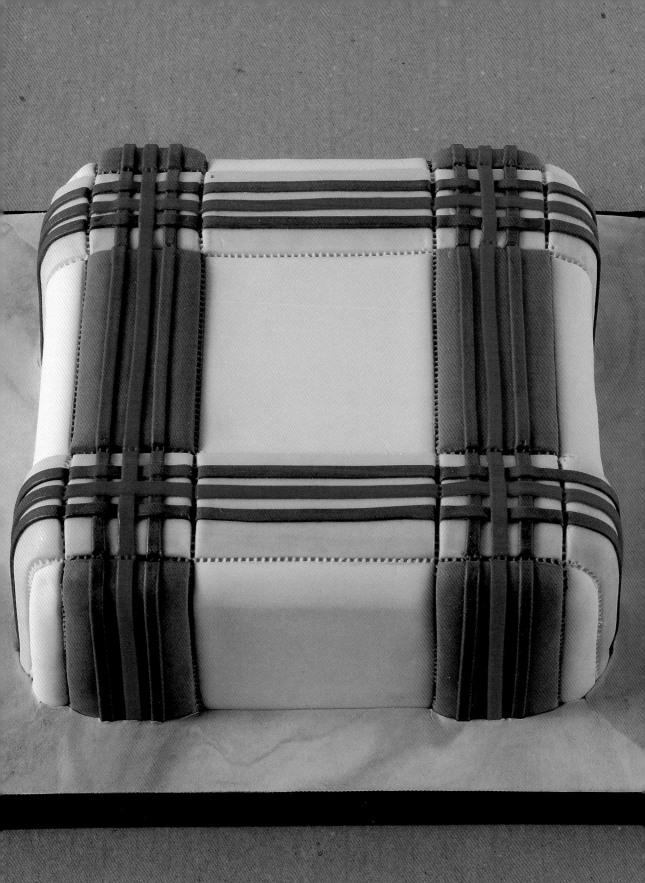

Quilting with Cutters

This alternative method of sugar quilting avoids piping designs on perspex, and is simpler for beginners.

Although limited by the number and shapes of cutters available, many designs are possible using varying combinations and numbers of cutters. With a little imagination and creativity, some interesting and attractive results can be produced, though this is necessarily a fairly freehand form of expression.

Planning

1 Cut out a piece of grease-proof paper the same size and shape as the top of the cake. Arrange the cutter or cutters on top of this to decide on the design. When you are satisfied, draw around the cutters. (Ready-drawn designs for the four examples that follow are given on pages 42–45. These can simply be traced on to a piece of paper and used as a guide for impressing the design.)

2 To transfer the design to the cake, place the pattern on the soft sugarpaste and press two or three cutters hard enough on the paper to impress the paste underneath. Remove the paper. The few outlines impressed will help you to arrange the rest of the cutter impressions correctly to create your design on the sugarpaste.

Techniques

3 The working method is exactly the same as detailed for the Blossom Cake (pages 7–11), except that cutters are used for the impressions and for cutting out the paste. The following four designs are examples for cake tops.

Teddy with Balloons

1 Cover the background with pale green sugarpaste and mark an impression with a large teddy bear cutter. Using the illustration on page 43 as a guide, impress three round balloons using a set of round briar rose cutters. Run lines of small stitches from the teddy's paw up to the three balloons, representing strings.

2 Use the small stitch wheel to impress tufts of grass around the teddy, and spray or dust this area in a darker green.

3 Using white royal icing of a thick run-sugar consistency, pipe the padding in the areas indicated by the dotted lines on the pattern (page 43). Leave to dry under a desk lamp.

4 Cut out the quilting pieces in appropriate colours of sugarpaste using the same cutters as before. Smooth down and moisten all the edges, and place over the padded areas. Small stitch all around.

5 Cut out and attach a small circle of paler paste for the teddy's muzzle, and indent a hole for the nose and two for the eyes. Fill these with tiny balls of black paste. Cover the foot pads with circles of paler paste, and indent each with three holes.

6 Use the small stitch wheel for the stitching on the teddy, and to define the outline of the head and body.

Butterfly and Blossoms

1 Cover the background with pale blue sugarpaste.

2 Trace the pattern (page 42) on to greaseproof paper, and impress the stems through the greaseproof paper on to the sugarpaste. Use this as a guide to arrange the rest of the design, making impressions with three sizes of blossom cutter, a large butterfly cutter and a leaf cutter.

3 Using white royal icing of a thick run-sugar consistency, pipe the padding in the areas indicated by the dotted lines on the pattern (page 42). Leave to dry under a desk lamp.

4 Cut out the quilting pieces in appropriate colours, using the same cutters. Smooth down and moisten the edges, and place over the padded areas. Small stitch all around.

5 Where the butterfly overlaps the flower, place the whole flower on first, then cut away the unwanted area by placing on the butterfly cutter and lining it up with the impression.

6 The butterfly is covered using paste coloured with paprika colouring. Cut out four small triangles of peach and overlay these on the wings. Use a no. 3 piping tube to cut out the tiny circles for the wing tips. Cut small rounds of brown paste and press into the blossom centres.

7 Small stitch around the edges and decorate all the pieces with extra stitching.

Poppies

1 Cover the background with white sugarpaste and make a tracing of the design on page 45. Use a round cutter to impress the centre of the large flower. Using medium poppy petal cutters, impress the petals around the centre.

2 Run a line of stitches down the design to indicate the stem of this flower, then impress the stem of the bud and the second flower in the same way. This will help you to decide the position of the leaves and the second flower.

3 Impress the top petal of the smaller flower using a small poppy petal cutter, then the centre, followed by the remaining petals. The large leaves are overlapped by the smaller flower, and the bud is impressed using the small petal cutter overlapping in three different directions.

4 Using white royal icing of a thick run-sugar consistency, pipe the padding in the areas indicated by the dotted lines on the pattern (page 45). (The leaves are not padded.) Leave to dry under a desk lamp.

5 Cut out the quilting pieces in the relevant colours, smooth and moisten the edges, and place on the design. Small stitch around them all, and use extra stitch lines for decoration.

Horseshoe

1 Cover the background with pale pink sugarpaste and impress the horseshoe using a large horseshoe cutter. Impress the larger blossom, overlapping the horseshoe at the base. Finish with the leaves and the smaller blossom.

2 Using white royal icing of a thick run-sugar consistency, pipe the padding in the areas indicated by the dotted lines on the pattern (page 44). Leave to dry.

3 Cut out quilting pieces in the relevant colours, smooth and moisten the edges, and place on the design. Place a small round piece of yellow paste in the centre of each flower. Small stitch around the edges, and use the stitch wheel to indent the veins on the leaves, the flower centres and petals, and the nail holes on the horseshoe.

Autumn Fruits

This would be suitable for celebrating Harvest Festival or a man's Birthday.
It incorporates a traditional rope design and marbled quilting.

Materials

Royal icing
23cm (9 inch) hexagonal cake
(measured point to point)
30cm (12 inch) hexagonal cake
board
1.25kg (2½ lb) marzipan (almond
paste)
1.25kg (2½ lb) sugarpaste (rolled
fondant)
Cream, green, red, brown and
yellow food colourings
Confectioners' varnish
Ribbon to trim board

Equipment

Piping bags
Nos. 1 and 1.5 piping tubes
(tips)
Small round cutter
7mm (⅓ inch) strip cutter
Wavy line crimper

Piping the designs

1 ⟩ Trace the top design (page 47), and pipe on to perspex using a no. 1.5 tube and white royal icing. Pipe the rope design on to perspex 1cm (½ inch) from the edge. Dry.

Quilting lines

2 ⟩ Place the cake on the board and cover with marzipan and then cream sugarpaste. Using a ruler, indent lines across the cake from point to point, creating six triangular sections. Extend these lines down the sides of the cake to the base. Large stitch all lines.

3 ⟩ Impress the top design, placing the pears in opposite triangular sections. On the sides, impress the rope by resting the edge of the perspex on the board so that the pattern starts 1cm (½ inch) from the base. Move the pattern around the cake, overlapping to create a continuous effect. Some slight adjustment may be necessary when finishing, depending on the size of the cake.

4 ⟩ Cover the board around the base of the cake with a strip of sugarpaste in the same way as for a round cake.

Padding

5 ⟩ Using white royal icing of a thick run-sugar consistency, pipe the padding on the top design in the areas indicated by the dotted lines on the pattern (page 47). Leave to dry under a desk lamp.

Quilting

6 ⟩ Prepare the sugarpaste for the top design quilting by colouring small amounts pale lemon, pale and medium green, light brown and red. For the large pears, lightly blend together some of the base cream sugarpaste and the medium green, creating a marbled effect. Roll this out and cover the pears, leaving the sugarpaste marbled.

7 ⟩ Cover the smaller pears in the pale green. Blend together a tiny amount of pink and brown. Roll this out thinly, cut small semi-circles and place one at the bottom of each small pear. Indent a hole at the base of each pear (large and small) with the end of a paintbrush. Small stitch around all the edges.

8 ⟩ Use the light brown, medium green and lemon

paste to cover the three leaves at the top of the pears. Small stitch around the edges and on top to represent veining.

9 To cover the three larger leaves grouped with the berries, use cream and lemon paste marbled together for the centre leaf, and green, light brown and lemon for the remaining two. Finish off with stitching in the same way as for the smaller leaves.

10 Cover the berries with red paste, using a small round cutter for a neater finish. Indent a hole in the base of each, opposite the stalk. Small stitch around the edges.

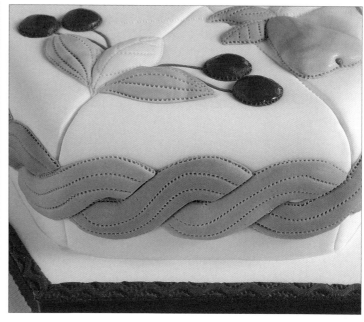

Rope

11 To quilt the rope on the side of the cake, colour some sugarpaste light brown and medium green. Roll out to 2.5mm (⅛ inch) thick, impress with the piped pattern, and cut out each section separately. Take great care when smoothing down the edges of these pieces before placing them on the cake, or you will find it difficult to fit them in. Attach to the cake, arranging the colours alternately. Small stitch the edges and run a pattern of two rows of stitches along the centre of each piece.

To complete

12 Cut strips of red paste using a strip cutter, and place these around the edge of the board. Crimp with a wavy line crimper.

13 Pipe the stalks of the berries in brown royal icing using a no. 1 tube, and a bulb in each indent at the base of the pears and berries. Paint the leaves, fruits and berries with confectioners' varnish. Trim the board with ribbon.

Floral Basket

This cake would be a real treat for Mother's Day, a Birthday or Easter.
The pattern is created using cutters (see page 24).

Materials

18cm (7 inch) round cake
25cm (10 inch) round cake board
1kg (2lb) marzipan (almond paste)
1kg (2lb) sugarpaste (rolled fondant)
Cream, yellow, orange, peach, brown and green food colourings
Royal icing
Ribbon to trim board

Equipment

Large petunia cutter
Leaf cutter
Closed-curve crimper
Piping bag
Basketweave rolling pin
Straight scallop-edged cutter

Preparation

1 Place the cake on the board and cover with marzipan and then with cream sugarpaste. Impress flowers and leaves at random on the top and slightly over the edge of the cake, using the large petunia and leaf cutters.

2 Cover the board around the base of the cake with a strip of paste. Trim to the edge of the board and crimp with a closed-curve crimper.

Padding

3 Using white royal icing of a thick run-sugar consistency, pipe the pads separately on the centres and petals of the flowers, and on the leaves. Do not pad any sections placed over the curved edge or on the side of the cake. Leave to dry.

Basketweave

4 Colour small amounts of sugarpaste yellow, orange, peach and green, and the remainder brown. Roll out the brown paste to 2.5mm (⅛ inch) thick and emboss with a basketweave rolling pin.

5 Cut the basketweave into strips 5cm (2 inches) deep, and scallop the top edge. Place these around the cake, making sure each join lies at the end of a scallop.

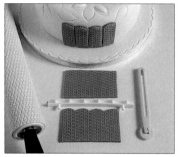

6 Large stitch along the top edge of the scallop and vertically down the basketweave between each one.

Quilting

7 Tint half the yellow, orange, peach and green paste with white paste to give two shades of each. Cut out the shapes using the same cutters as for the impressions, and smooth the edges. Moisten and position over the padded areas.

8 Small stitch all around the edges, and in lines radiating from the centres of the flowers. Vein the leaves.

9 Cut out small brown circles for the centres of the flowers, attach and crisscross with small stitches. Trim the board with ribbon.

Bells and Bows

Shown here as a Christmas cake, this design would also be suitable for a wedding or anniversary. The special techniques required include quilting round sharp corners.

Materials

Royal icing
25cm (10 inch) triangular cake
36cm (14 inch) triangular cake board
1.25kg (2½ lb) marzipan (almond paste)
1.25kg (2½ lb) sugarpaste (rolled fondant)
Red, lemon and egg yellow food colourings
Confectioners' varnish
Red ribbon to trim board

Equipment

Piping bags
No. 1.5 piping tube (tip)
Glue stick

Piping the design

 1 Trace the top bells and bow design (page 41), and pipe in the centre of a piece of perspex, using a no. 1.5 piping tube and white royal icing. Pipe the corner bow design 5mm (¼ inch) from the edge of another, smaller piece of perspex. Leave to dry.

Quilting lines

2 Place the cake on the cake board, and cover the cake with marzipan, then with white sugarpaste.

3 Place a ruler along one edge on top of the cake and indent a line approximately 1cm (½ inch) inwards. Continue making parallel lines across the cake, spacing them the ruler's width apart. Repeat this process, starting at a second edge of the cake.

4 The third set of lines should be impressed parallel to the remaining edge, and should be positioned so that all three sets of lines cross at the same places, making triangular shapes in the sugarpaste on top of the cake.

5 Continue the quilting lines over the edge of the cake until they form points, then mark a horizontal line around the sides of the cake joining all the points together. Extend one of the diagonals from each point down to the base of the cake, choosing the same diagonal in each case to create parallels all around. On the corners, extend the lines straight down on each side. Run the large stitch wheel along all the quilting lines on the top and sides of the cake.

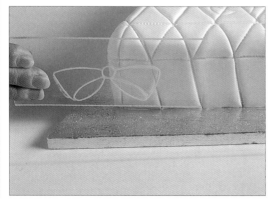
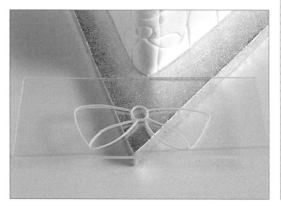

end of the quilting tool to indent between. Small stitch around the edges and across the base, 1cm (½ inch) from the edge.

<13> On the corner bows, apply thinly rolled paste to the insides of the loops, and thicker paste to the remainder, as on the top of the cake, except that there is no padding underneath.

<14> Leave all the quilting to dry, then brush the red bows with confectioners' varnish.

Ribbon and bows

<15> Attach a red ribbon all around the edge of the board, using a glue stick to secure. To make the bows, cut a 30cm (12 inch) length of ribbon into three lengths of 20cm (8 inches), 4cm (1½ inches) and 6cm (2½ inches). Fold the longest piece inwards from each end to meet in the centre, forming loops. Cut a triangle at both ends of the 6cm (2½ inch) piece and stick this on top. Use the shortest piece to fold around the centre and form the knot. Secure a bow halfway along each side of the board.

<6> Impress the top of the cake with the bell and bow design. To mark the corner bows, rest the edge of the perspex on the board and rock from side to side, round the corner, to ensure the design is complete on both sides.

<7> Cover the board around the cake with strips of white sugarpaste, joining at each corner, from the point of the board to the point of the cake. Smooth over the joins carefully and leave to dry.

Padding

<8> Using white royal icing of a thick run-sugar consistency, pipe the pads on the top bells and bows in the areas indicated by the dotted lines on the pattern (page 41). Leave to dry under a desk lamp.

Quilting

<9> Colour a small amount of sugarpaste red for the bows, and for the bells make golden coloured paste by mixing lemon and egg yellow.

<10> Commence the quilting with the insides of the bow loops, which are not padded. Roll out the paste thinly, impress the perspex pattern, and cut out. Round off the edges, moisten and attach to the cake.

<11> Cover the rest of the bow in the usual manner with 2.5mm (⅛ inch) thick paste. Small stitch around the edges and use the stitch wheel to give the impression of pleats in the ribbon.

<12> Cover the bells separately. Leave the clapper on each one and use the veining

Christmas Snowman

This Christmas cake with a difference is finished with simple piped lettering and a frosted 'snow' effect.

Materials

Royal icing
20cm (8 inch) round cake
28cm (11 inch) round cake board
1kg (2lb) marzipan (almond paste)
1kg (2lb) sugarpaste (rolled fondant)
Red, green and brown food colourings
Blue petal dust (blossom tint)
Ribbon to trim board

Equipment

Piping bags
Nos. 1.5, 2 and 3 piping tubes (tips)
Large ball tool
7mm (⅓ inch) strip cutter
Small holly leaf crimper

Piping the designs

1 Trace the snowman design (page 46) on to a 20cm (8 inch) disc of greaseproof paper. Place face up on a piece of perspex, securing with tape. Turn the perspex over and pipe the lettering and snowman's stick in white royal icing with a no. 2 tube, and the rest of the design with a no. 1.5 tube. (You will be piping the lettering back to front on to the perspex.)

2 Pipe the snowball side design (page 46) 1cm (½ inch) from the edge of another, smaller piece of perspex. Leave the piped patterns to dry.

Quilting lines

3 Place the cake on the cake board and cover with marzipan and then with white sugarpaste. Lay a paper template on the top of the cake (page 8), and mark two lines at 90° to each other across the centre.

4 Impress the rest of the lines parallel to the first two, spacing them the ruler's width apart and finishing slightly over the edge of the cake. Join the ends of the lines to create squares.

5 Impress the top design over the quilting lines. When positioning, make sure that none of the lettering lies along a groove of the quilting. Large stitch the quilting grooves, avoiding the picture.

6 Impress the side design by overlapping the pattern as you work around the cake, rocking the perspex from side to side to form a continuous snowball pattern. Some adjustment may be needed where you finish, depending on the circumference of the cake.

7 Cover the board around the cake with a strip of white sugarpaste and impress small hollows around the edge with a large ball tool. Leave to dry.

Padding and lettering

8 Pipe the lettering in red with a no. 1.5 tube.

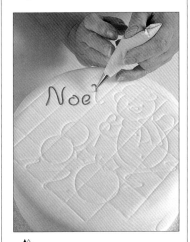

9 Using white royal icing of a thick run-sugar consistency, pipe the pads on the top design in the areas indicated by the dotted lines on the pattern

(page 46). Leave to dry under a desk lamp.

Quilting

10 Roll out some white paste and cut out pieces for covering the snowman first. Apply the red scarf over the top. Cover the hat in brown and insert tiny balls of brown paste in the eyes and buttons. Small stitch around every section and inside the groove of the mouth. Make a small indent for the nose and insert a small, slightly flattened ball of paste.

11 Cover the three top snowballs in white, cutting each one out separately. Small stitch around the edges. Cover the holly leaves and small stitch around the edges and on top for veins.

12 For the side of the cake, roll out white paste to 5mm (¼ inch) thick, mark on the pattern with the perspex, and cut out and apply each snowball separately, finishing around the edges with small stitches as you proceed. Impress a semi-circular line of stitches at the top of each one about 5mm (¼ inch) from the edge.

To complete

13 To finish round the bottom of the cake, attach 7mm (⅓ inch) strips of green paste and crimp using a small holly crimper. Cut out some red berries using a no. 3 piping tube, and arrange around the green strip, and with the holly leaves on the top of the cake.

14 Pipe the walking stick in red with a no. 1.5 tube.

15 Mix some blue petal dust with cornflour and, with a small brush, dust around the edges of the snowman and the snowballs, top and sides, to make them stand out from the white background. Dust in the hollows on the edge of the board.

16 Place some white royal icing in a piping bag without a tube, and snip off the end to make a small hole. Pipe along the squiggly lines below the top picture, and pipe at random on the snowman's hat and arms, over the top of each snowball and on the holly leaves. Spread the icing using a small paintbrush and sprinkle with granulated sugar while it is still wet. Leave to dry, then turn the cake upside-down over a piece of greaseproof paper to remove and collect the excess sugar. Finally, trim the cake board with a length of ribbon.

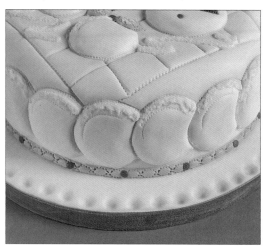

Wedding Cake

This design can be presented unadorned or enhanced with sprays of flowers. The heart plaques could be replaced with alternative decorations, such as monograms.

Materials

Flower paste
4.5kg (10lb) sugarpaste (rolled fondant)
Pink petal dust (blossom tint)
Royal icing
15x20cm (6x8 inch), 20x25cm (8x10 inch), 25x30cm (10x12 inch) oval cakes
23x28cm (9x11 inch), 28x33cm (11x13 inch), 33x38cm (13x15 inch) oval cake boards
4kg (9lb) marzipan (almond paste)
3 posy picks, optional
Ivory and pink food colourings
Edible glue
Ribbon to trim boards
Flower sprays, optional

Equipment

4cm (1½ inch), 5cm (2 inch) round cutters
Small heart-shaped cutters (2 sizes)
Piping bags
No. 1.5 piping tube (tip)
3mm (⅛ inch) strip cutter
Perspex cake stand

Plaques

1 Mix a paste from equal quantities of flower paste and sugarpaste. Roll out very thinly and cut out two 4cm (1½ inch) and four 5cm (2 inch) rounds. (The smaller plaques are for the top tier, and the larger for the middle and bottom tiers.) Place on a board and leave to dry.

2 Lighten some pink petal dust by mixing with cornflour, and dust in the centre of each plaque, rubbing it into the surface and leaving a small margin of white around the edge. Place the plaques, one at a time, upside-down in a metal sieve and pass through a jet of steam. This will fix the colour.

3 Two sizes of heart cutter are needed to correspond with the two sizes of plaque. To make sure they will fit, draw around the cutters, cut out and overlap the drawings. Try them in position over the relevant plaque.

4 Roll out some ivory sugarpaste to 5mm (¼ inch) thick, and cut out two hearts for each plaque, using a larger cutter for the larger plaques. Overlap two same-size hearts and use the relevant cutter to remove the unwanted section from the one underneath. Smooth down the edges and attach to the plaques. Small stitch around the edges of both hearts on each plaque.

Shells

5 Enlarge the shell pattern as required (page 44), trace, and pipe the three outlines on three separate pieces of perspex, using white royal icing and a no. 1.5 tube. (Check the sizes of the patterns before purchasing the perspex sheets.) Enlarge and pipe the side shell designs (page 45) 5mm (¼ inch) from the edge of three smaller sheets of perspex. Leave to dry.

6 Place the cakes on the cake boards and cover with marzipan and then with ivory sugarpaste. (You can colour this yourself, but for such a large quantity it is easier to purchase it ready coloured.)

7 Impress the top designs, then the side designs by resting the edge of the perspex sheet on the board each time to ensure the correct gap at the base.

8 If you intend to decorate the tops of the cakes with sprays of flowers, insert a posy pick into the top of each cake behind the curved end of the shell. This will enable you to arrange the flowers across the narrow end of the design.

Positioning plaques

9 Cut out round holes for the plaques on the sides of the cakes, using the 5cm (2 inch) cutter for the bottom and middle tiers, and the 4cm (1½ inch) cutter for the top tier. These should be placed centrally between the shell designs and in line with their bases. Press the cutters into the paste and remove the circles. Slot in the plaques. (Leave the cut edges raw; these will be lined with pink at a later stage.)

10 Cover the boards around the cakes with strips of ivory sugarpaste. Leave to dry.

Padding

11 Using white royal icing of a thick run-sugar consistency, pipe the padding on the top design of each cake within the areas indicated by the dotted lines on the pattern (page 44). Dry under a desk lamp.

Quilting

12 Roll out the paste for the quilting and impress the top shell design. Cut this out in two sections along the centre depression to make covering easier. Smooth down and moisten all the edges, and work the inside scallops of the shell first. Carefully smooth down to the surface of the cake, using the impressed line as a guide for the shape. Press down lightly between the two scallops and run the veining end of the quilting tool along this line to create a definite division. Small stitch around all the edges, along the dividing line and lengthways halfway across each section. Repeat this process for the two outside scallops.

13 For the side quilting, roll out the paste to 2.5mm (⅛ inch) thick, impress the piped design, and cut out each set of three scallops in one piece. Smooth down the edges and vein between the scallops for clearer definition. Moisten and attach to the cake, and small stitch in the same way as the top design.

To complete

14 To line the inside edges of the plaques, cut some 3mm (⅛ inch) strips of pink flower paste, place inside the edge and attach with edible glue. Trim the boards with ribbon. Arrange the flowers, if using, in the posy picks, and place the cakes on the stand.

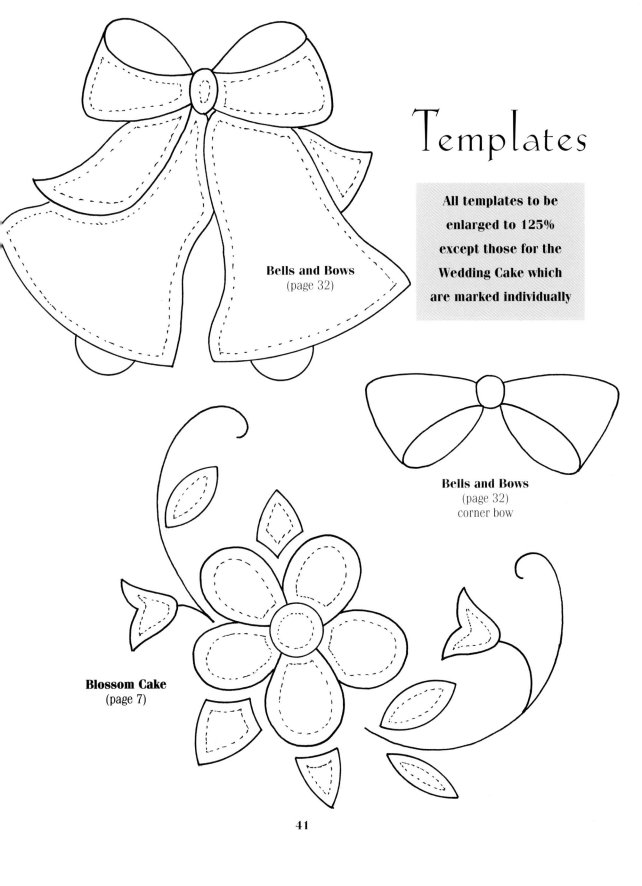

Templates

All templates to be enlarged to 125% except those for the Wedding Cake which are marked individually

Bells and Bows
(page 32)

Bells and Bows
(page 32)
corner bow

Blossom Cake
(page 7)

Butterfly and Blossoms
(page 25)

Ribbons and Bows
(page 15)
side tails

All templates
to be enlarged
to 125%
except those
for the
Wedding Cake
which are
marked
individually

Ribbons and Bows
(page 15)

42

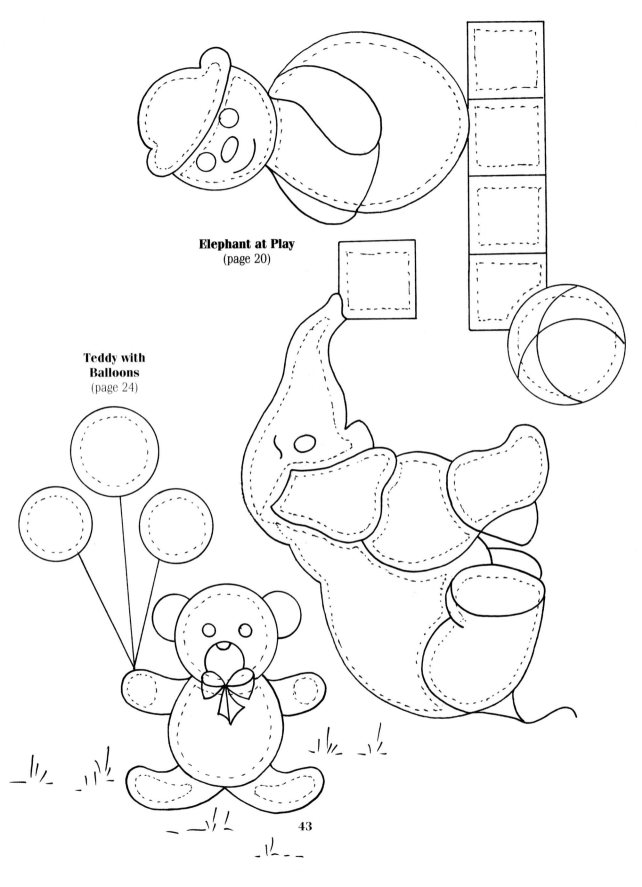

Elephant at Play
(page 20)

**Teddy with
Balloons**
(page 24)

43

Wedding Cake
(page 38)
top tier shell design (actual size)
for middle tier enlarge to 125%
for bottom tier enlarge to 130%

Horseshoe
(page 26)

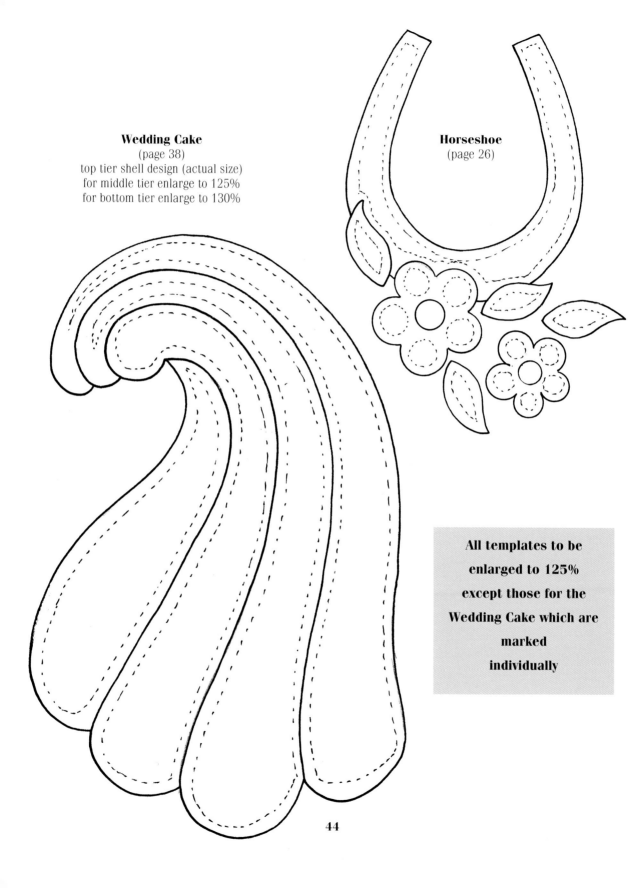

All templates to be
enlarged to 125%
except those for the
Wedding Cake which are
marked
individually

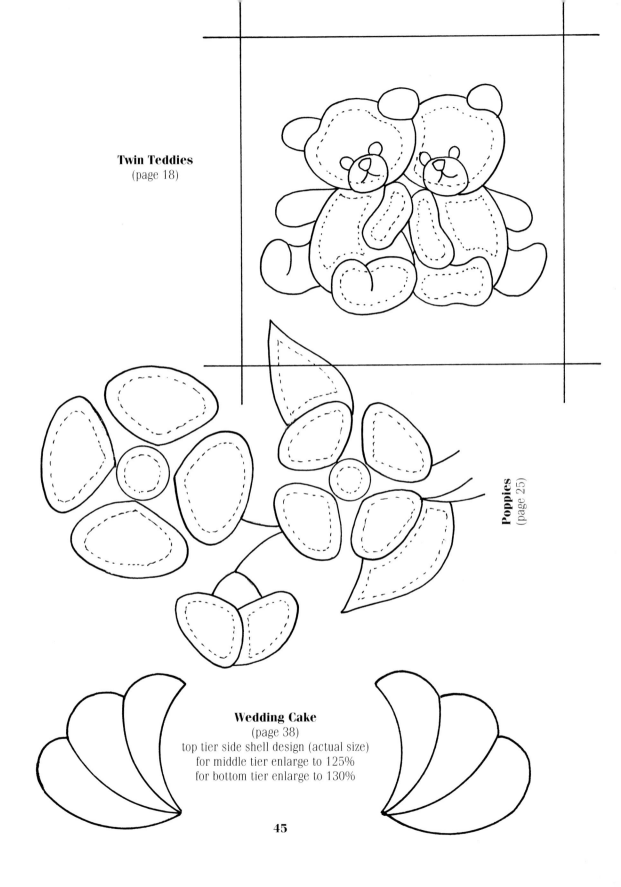

Twin Teddies
(page 18)

Poppies
(page 25)

Wedding Cake
(page 38)
top tier side shell design (actual size)
for middle tier enlarge to 125%
for bottom tier enlarge to 130%

Noel

Christmas Snowman
(page 35)

Orchid Cake
(page 12)

Christmas Snowman
(page 35)
side snowball design

46

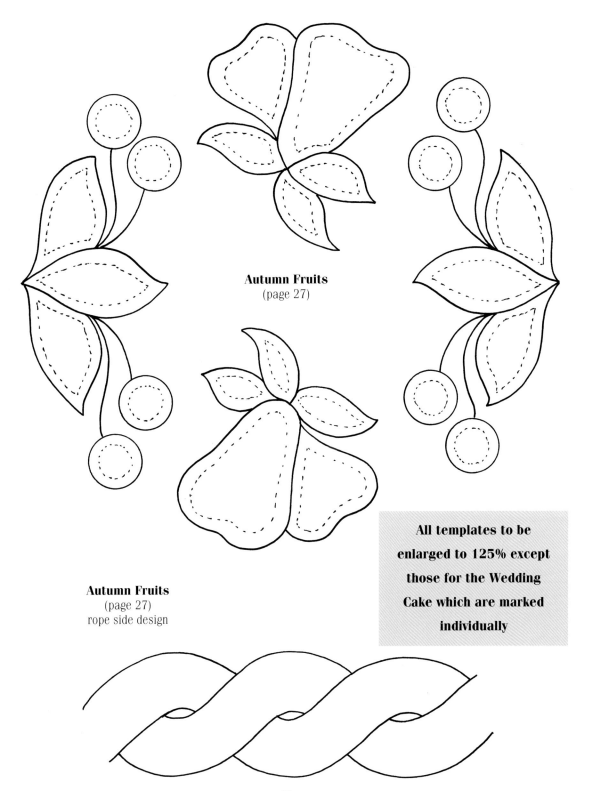

Autumn Fruits
(page 27)

Autumn Fruits
(page 27)
rope side design

All templates to be enlarged to 125% except those for the Wedding Cake which are marked individually

Acknowledgements

Special thanks to my husband, Bruce, for all his help and support. Thanks also to Patricia Harrison for her help and expertise.

The author and publishers would like to thank the following suppliers:

E.T. Webb
(dummies)
18 Meadow Close,
Woodley,
Stockport SK6 1QZ

J. F. Renshaw Ltd.
(Regalice)
Crown Street,
Liverpool L8 7RF

Sugar Celebrations
176A Manchester Road,
Swindon SN1 1TU

P.M.E. Sugarcraft
Brember Road,
South Harrow HA2 8UN

Tinkertech Two
40 Langdon Road,
Parkstone,
Poole,
Dorset BH14 9EH

Cake Art Ltd.
Venture Way,
Crown Estate,
Priorswood,
Taunton,
Devon TA2 8DE

Guy, Paul & Co. Ltd.
Unit B4,
Foundry Way,
Little End Road,
Eaton Socon,
Cambs. PE19 3JH

Squires Kitchen
Squires House,
3 Waverley Lane,
Farnham,
Surrey GU9 8BB

Anniversary House (Cake Decorations) Ltd.
Unit 5,
Roundways,
Elliott Road,
Bournemouth BH11 8JJ